What Is A Solar System

By Theodore W. Munch, Ed. D.

Professor of Science Education   University of Arizona

Pictures — Berthold Tiedemann

BENEFIC PRESS · CHICAGO

Publishing Division of Beckley-Cardy Company

Atlanta 3, Georgia   Dallas 1, Texas
Long Beach 3, California   Portland 4, Oregon

The WHAT IS IT Series

What Is A Plant

What Is A Season

What Is A Turtle

What Is A Bird

What Is A Chicken

What Is A Fish

What Is A Butterfly

What Is A Cow

What Is A Frog

What Is A Tree

What Is A Rock

What Is A Magnet

What Is A Rocket

What Is A Solar System

What Is A Machine

What Is Light

What Is Air

What Is Gravity

What Is Weather

What Is Electricity

What Is Water

What Is Sound

What Is A Star

Library of Congress
Number 59-12334

CONTENTS

THIS IS A SOLAR SYSTEM

A solar system is a sun and all the heavenly bodies which move around it.

The word "solar" means sun.

In our solar system, there are six different kinds of heavenly bodies.

1. The sun is really a medium-sized star. It gives off its own light. The sun makes up 99% of our entire solar system in size and amount of material it contains.

Mercury Venus Earth Mars Planetoids Jupiter Saturn Uranus

2. The earth is a planet. Nine planets travel around the sun. A planet gives off no light of its own.

3. Thirty-one moons in all travel around six of the planets. The other three planets have no moons.

4. Thousands of small planetoids are between the planets Mars and Jupiter.

5. Comets are great collections of loose dust and rock particles. They form long tails when they travel near the sun.

6. Meteors are single rock fragments which travel through our solar system.

Neptune

Pluto

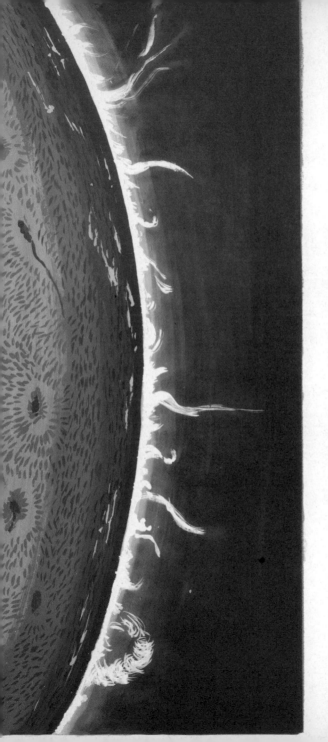

Our solar system is shaped like a huge oval billions of miles across. Like horses on a merry-go-round, the planets travel around the sun in oval paths. Each planet is a different distance from the sun.

The planet Mercury is closest to the sun at a distance of 36,000,000 miles.

Pluto, 4,000,000,000 miles from the sun, is farthest away.

The earth is fairly close at a distance of 93,000,000 miles from the sun.

The pictures on these two pages show how large the planets would be if the sun were about the size of a two-foot beach ball.

Jupiter and Saturn are the largest. Neptune and Uranus are next, each about 30,000 miles across. Earth and Venus are about 8,000 miles across. Mars, 4,100 miles across, and Pluto and Mercury, about 3,100 miles across, are the smallest planets.

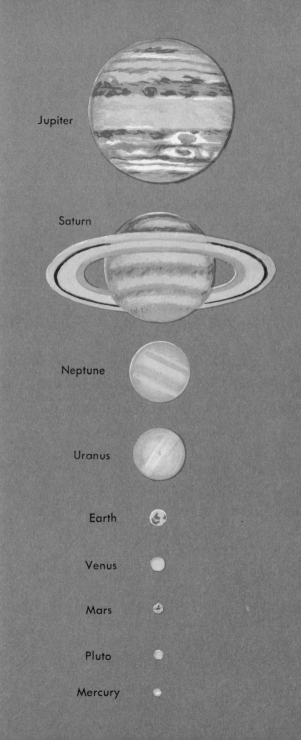

Jupiter

Saturn

Neptune

Uranus

Earth

Venus

Mars

Pluto

Mercury

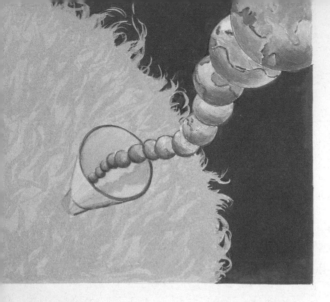

Compared with the sun, the planets are tiny. The sun weighs about 700 times as much as all the rest of the solar system combined.

If the sun were hollow, over a million earths could be poured into it.

It would take about 332,000 earths to balance the weight of the sun.

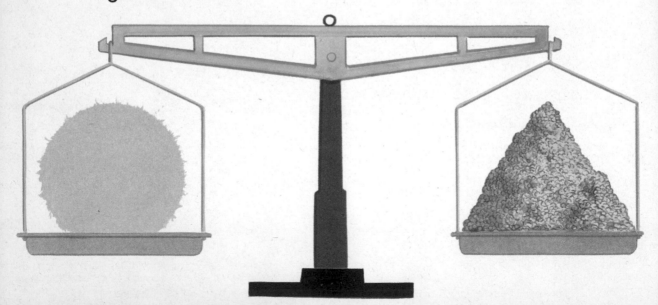

Even if the planets and the sun were the same size, they would not weigh the same. The reason for this is that the planets are made of different materials.

The sun consists of gas. We think of gas as being something like air. Planets like the earth are made of solid matter.

These pictures show how the weight of the sun and some of the planets and our moon would compare to a ball of water the same size.

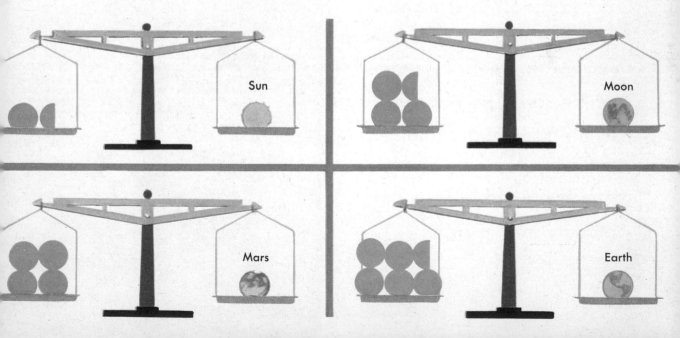

The word planet means "wanderer." But planets do not wander just any direction in space. They move in exact and orderly orbits around the sun. An orbit is the path of a planet around the sun.

All of the planets are moving so fast that they would fly off in straight lines through space if it were not for the pull of gravity of the sun. The outward pull of the speeding planets and the pull of gravity of the sun are equal in force. The planets stay in orbit.

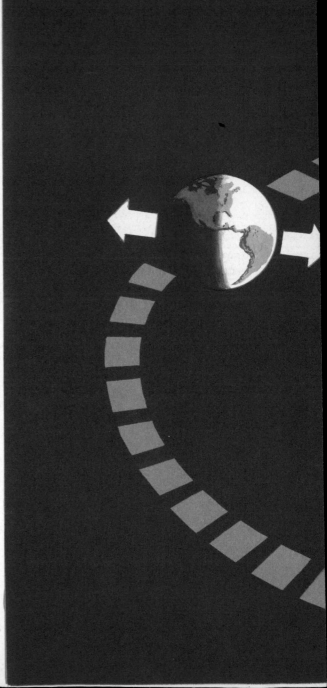

The earth would fly out into space if it were not pulled toward the sun by the force of gravity.

STUDYING OUR SOLAR SYSTEM

In order to learn about our
solar system, scientists use
special tools. One of these
tools is the telescope. A
scientist can see far into
space when he looks
through a telescope.

Scientists use
the radio telescope.
This tool can pick
up radio waves from
the sun and planets.

The spectroscope
can tell scientists
what chemicals are
in the atmosphere
of the stars and
planets. The gases
which surround a
star or a planet
make up its
atmosphere.

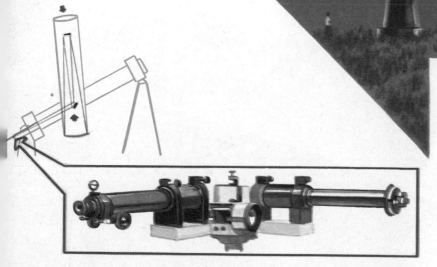

THE SUN, POWERHOUSE OF THE SOLAR SYSTEM

Of all the stars, none is as important to us as our sun.
Without heat and light from the sun, our earth would be
a cold lifeless ball of rock and ice.

The bright surface of the sun looks like a stormy sea
when it is seen through a special instrument. Great
explosions of flaming gases on the sun
shoot huge streams thousands
of miles out from its
surface.

The temperature on the surface of the sun is about 10,000 degrees Fahrenheit. Scientists estimate that the temperature at the center of the sun may be as high as 32,000,000 degrees F. Even the hardest materials on earth would be turned into hot gases at temperatures as hot as this. The sun must use about 4,200,000 tons of itself every second to keep burning. But the sun probably will burn billions of years more.

With the help of the spectroscope, scientists have found many of the elements known on earth to be in the hot gases of the sun. There are only 92 elements in nature. All matter known to man is made of one or more of these elements.

The most important elements in the sun are hydrogen and helium. These make up almost all of the gases of the sun.

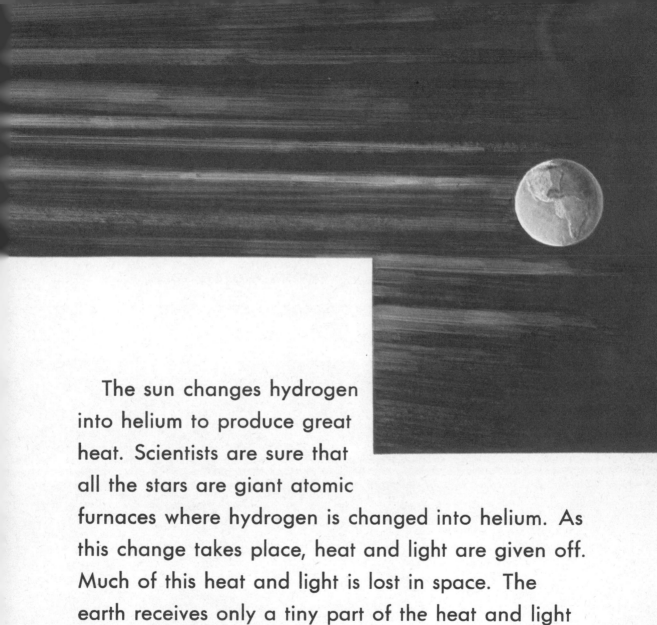

The sun changes hydrogen into helium to produce great heat. Scientists are sure that all the stars are giant atomic furnaces where hydrogen is changed into helium. As this change takes place, heat and light are given off. Much of this heat and light is lost in space. The earth receives only a tiny part of the heat and light rays from the sun.

Dark areas called sunspots appear regularly on the face of the sun. They grow large quickly and then disappear. The greatest number of sunspots to appear at any one time can be seen about every eleven years.

Soon after large sunspots appear, a shower of atomic particles reaches the earth.

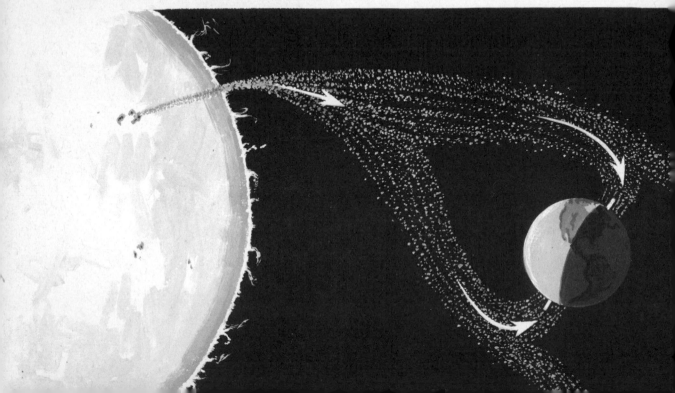

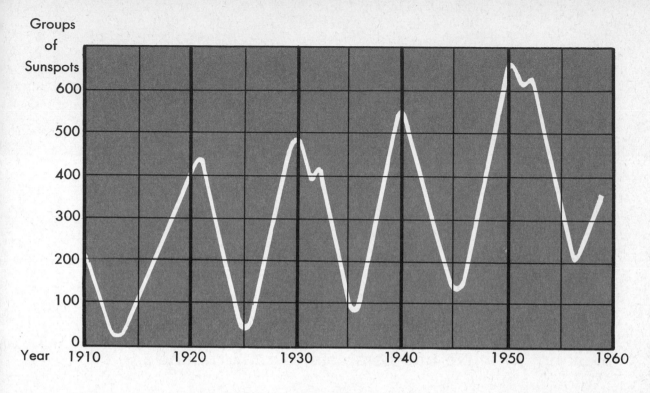

Atomic particles from sunspots can affect a number of things on earth. The particles cause magnetic storms on earth. Radio, telegraph, and long distance telephone signals can fade out or become mixed up.

Sunspots may affect the weather. The temperature has often dropped after sunspots appeared.

The picture on this page shows the number of sunspot groups counted during the years 1900 to 1958.

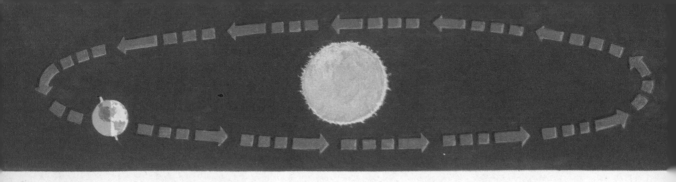

NIGHTS, DAYS, AND SEASONS ON THE PLANETS

The sun is the center of our solar system with all the planets circling it. We say that the planets revolve around the sun. The amount of time that it takes a planet to make one complete journey around the sun

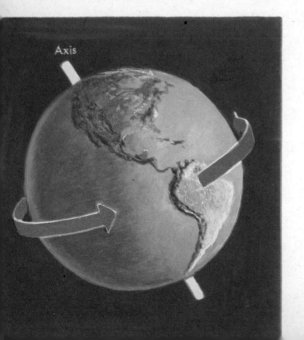

Axis

is a year on that planet.

Most of the planets also rotate on their axes while they revolve around the sun. This means that a planet spins around an imaginary line through its center. The axis of the earth is tilted.

It is the rotation of the planets that causes night and day. As the earth rotates, one side is always turned away from the sun. The side that is toward the sun is having daylight. The side that is turned away from the sun is having night.

Earth and Mars rotate once every 24 hours. The planets Jupiter, Saturn, and Uranus rotate once in less than twelve hours. The days and nights are much shorter on these planets than on Earth and Mars.

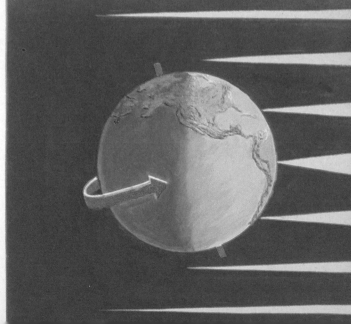

The earth and some of the other planets have four seasons each year because of the tilt of their axes.

In North America, summer comes when the axis of the earth is tilted toward the sun. Summer days are warm because the direct rays of the sun reach this area of the earth. In summer, days are longer than the nights.

Winter comes to North America when the earth is at the opposite end of its orbit. Now the axis is tilted away from the sun. Winter days are cold because the direct rays of the sun cannot reach this area. The days are shorter than the nights.

During spring and autumn, the axis of the earth is not tilted either toward or away from the sun. During these seasons, the Equator receives the direct and hottest rays of the sun.

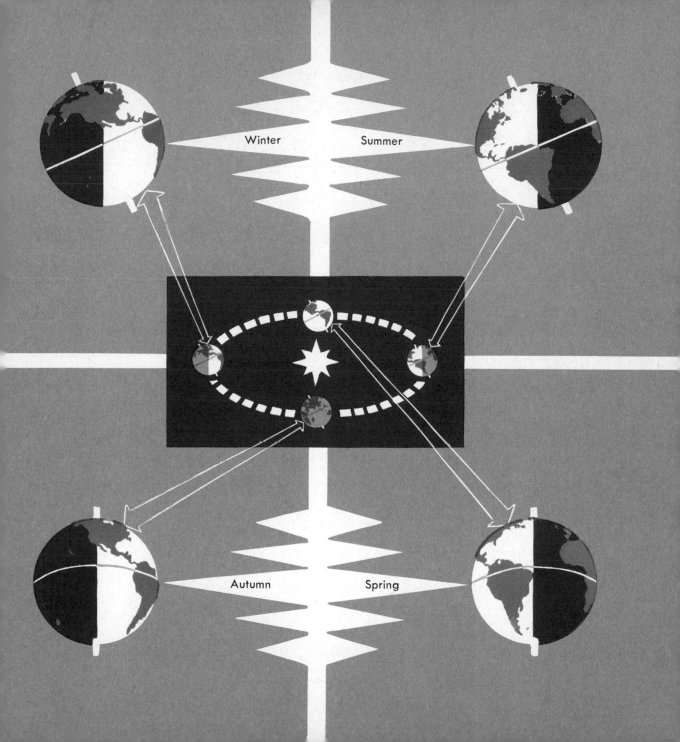

Winter   Summer

Autumn   Spring

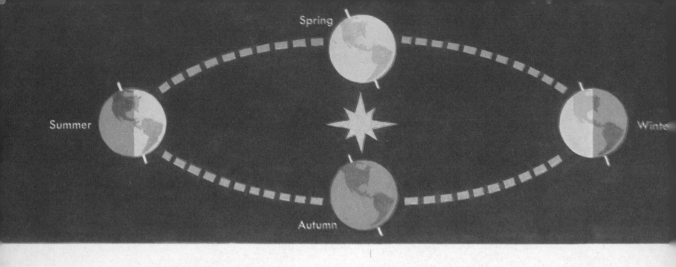

The seasons of South America come at opposite times from the seasons of North America. When it is summer in North America, it is winter in South America. South America is receiving only indirect rays from the sun at this time. When it is spring in North America, it is autumn in South America.

Two planets, Mercury and Venus, are not tilted on their axes. There are no seasons on these planets. Mars is tilted about the same way as the earth and seasons are probably similar. Jupiter is tilted slightly. The seasons probably change very little on Jupiter.

24

EARTH, THE MOST IMPORTANT PLANET

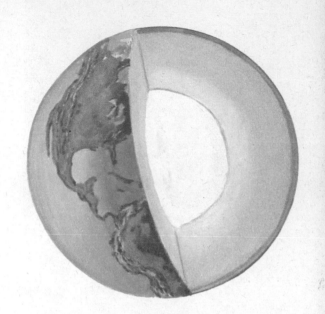

Our planet, the earth, is a huge ball. If we could slice a section from it, we would find around the outside of the earth a crust about 25 or 30 miles thick.

Beneath this crust is a sea of hot, liquid rock 2,000 miles thick. A core of nickel and iron makes up the center of the earth.

Most of the surface of the earth is covered by oceans. The ocean floors are made up of mountains and plains.

Surrounding the earth is
a blanket of air, or the
atmosphere. The atmosphere
is hundreds of miles thick.
Most living things exist
within the first ten miles of it.

This blanket of air provides us with the oxygen
we breathe, the water we drink, and with protection
from harmful rays of the sun.

Circling the
earth is our
nearest space
neighbor, the
moon. It is
only 239,000
miles away.

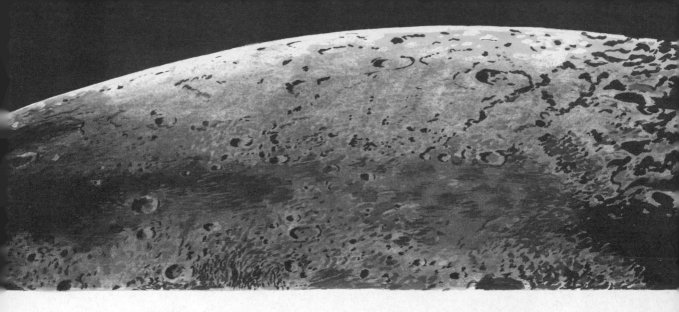

Through a telescope, our moon shows itself to be a huge ball of rock covered with craters, mountain ranges, and wide plains. Early scientists thought the plains were seas to which they gave unusual names.

The moon is held in orbit by the earth, just as the earth is held by the sun. The moon takes about twenty-nine days to make one trip around the earth.

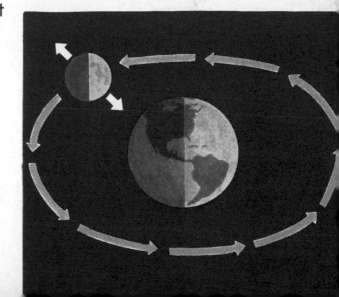

The pull of gravity is only one-sixth of that on earth. We could leap and jump long distances on the moon.

There is not even enough gravity to hold air and water on the moon. It never rains or snows. Not a sound is heard.

Only one-half of the moon is exposed to the sun at any one time. We can see the moon when its lighted side is toward the earth. We cannot see the moon when it is between the earth and the sun because only its dark side is toward us. We say that the moon is new when its dark side is toward us.

As the moon travels around the earth, more and more of its lighted side turns toward us. When the moon is half-way through its orbit, all of its lighted side is toward the earth. We say the moon is full. Then it grows smaller and smaller until we cannot see it.

These changes in the moon are called the phases of the moon.

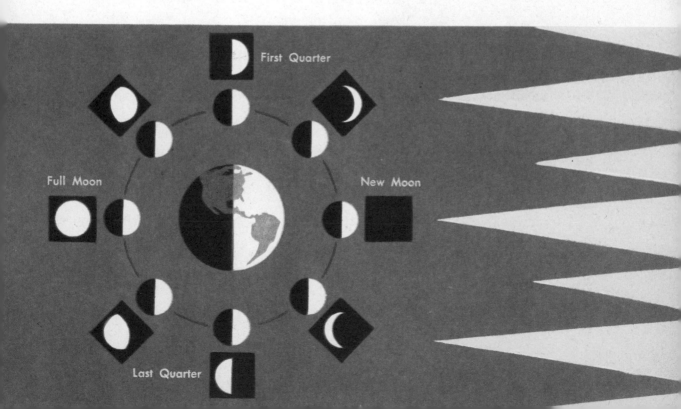

VENUS, TWIN TO THE EARTH

The planet Venus is one of the most beautiful in our solar system. It shines so brightly that at times we can see it during daylight.

Venus and Earth are both about the same size, and both contain about the same amount of material. The pull of gravity is a little less on Venus, but we could easily walk around on it.

No one has ever seen the surface of Venus because it is surrounded by heavy gas. Some scientists think Venus may be a dry desert. Others believe that under the clouds, Venus may be covered with water.

The orbit of Venus is closer to the sun than the orbit of the earth. It completes one trip every 225 days.

Venus shows all the phases of our moon. When it is closest, it looks like a long, thin moon. When it is farthest away, it looks like a small full moon.

We see Venus sometimes in the morning and sometimes in the evening. It is often called the morning star or the evening star.

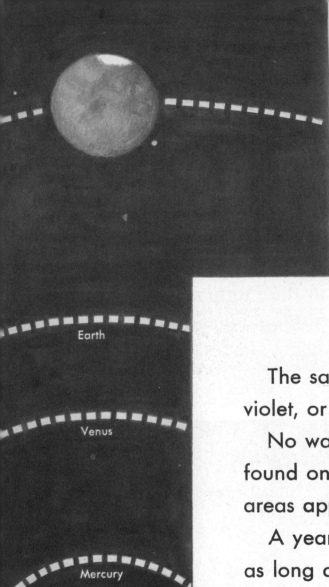

MARS . . .

DOES LIFE EXIST THERE?

Mars is often called the "Red Planet." More than half of its surface is brick-red color. Some areas appear blue, green, or gray in the winter.

The same areas are brown, violet, or red in the summer.

No water or oxygen has been found on Mars, but the polar areas appear to have ice and snow.

A year on Mars is almost twice as long as a year on earth. Day and night on Mars are almost exactly the same as on Earth. Mars is only one-half the size of the earth.

Many scientists report that they have seen canals on Mars through a telescope. But these canals have never shown in a photograph.

Some scientists believe the canals could have been made by Martian people. Others say that the canals are just large cracks on the surface of the planet.

It is possible that very simple plants, called lichens, and some tiny animals live on rocks or in the ground. Even though Mars is far away from the sun, its temperature sometimes rises to 80 degrees. But without water or oxygen, life, as we know it, probably doesn't exist.

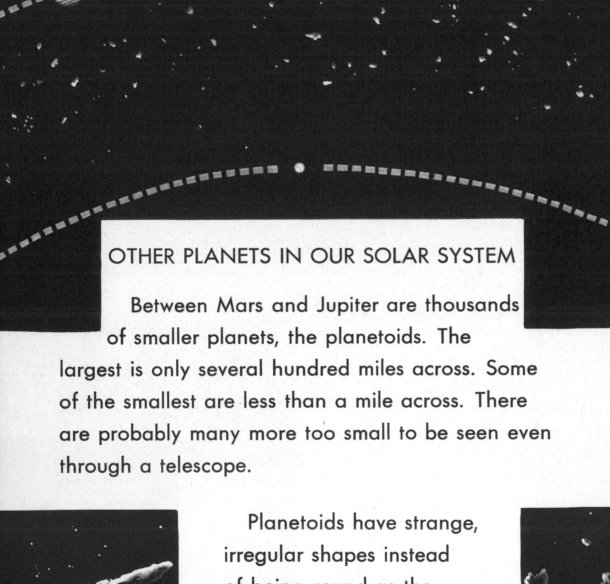

OTHER PLANETS IN OUR SOLAR SYSTEM

Between Mars and Jupiter are thousands of smaller planets, the planetoids. The largest is only several hundred miles across. Some of the smallest are less than a mile across. There are probably many more too small to be seen even through a telescope.

Planetoids have strange, irregular shapes instead of being round as the planets are.

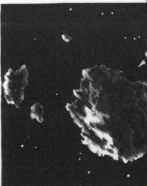

Mercury is the
smallest and travels
fastest of the nine
planets. It could
rest in the
Atlantic Ocean
without touching
on either side.

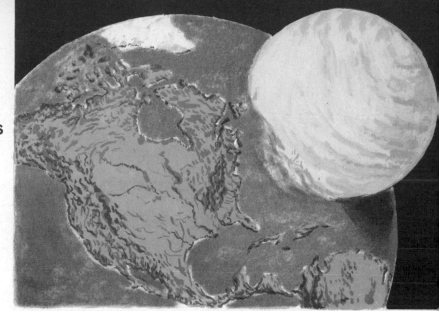

Mercury travels so fast that it revolves around the
sun in just 88 days.

Mercury rotates once on its axis while revolving
around the sun. This means that the same side is
always toward the sun.
This side is hot enough to
melt lead. The other side
is always dark and has
temperatures many hundreds
of degrees below zero.

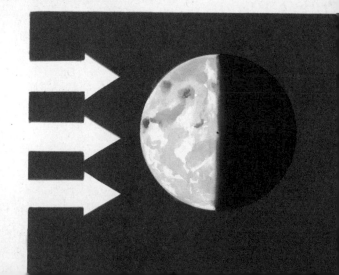

Jupiter, giant of all the planets, is so huge that all of the other planets could be put into it and there would still be room to spare.

Jupiter is covered with thick clouds which change their color from time to time. Near the pole is a large spot which often appears pink in a telescope. It is called the Great Red Spot.

Jupiter has twelve moons, the most of any planet.

There probably is no life on Jupiter. The atmosphere is poisonous, and the temperature is about 200 degrees below zero.

Saturn, second largest of the planets, is the
showpiece of the solar system. Wheeling around its
equator are three colorful rings, each of which is
thousands of miles across. The rings are probably
not more than ten miles thick. Some scientists believe
the rings are made of tiny particles of rock from
some shattered moon that came too close to the
planet. Recently, one famous scientist reported that
he believed the rings to be snow crystals.

Sometimes the rings of Saturn seem to disappear. The rings are still there. The planet has only moved in its orbit so that the rings are viewed edgewise from the earth. In this position, the rings can be seen with only the largest telescope.

Saturn is so far from the sun that it receives only about 1/1000 as much sunlight as the earth. The temperature is very low. Saturn is also surrounded by clouds of gas which would be poisonous to living things on earth.

Uranus and Neptune might be considered twins in the solar system. Each is about 30,000 miles across. The pull of gravity is about the same on each planet. Both are surrounded by clouds of poisonous gas and both are extremely cold.

Uranus is different from all other planets in the way its axis is tilted. Instead of being tilted slightly as the earth, Uranus is tilted so that it is rolling along as a top on its side.

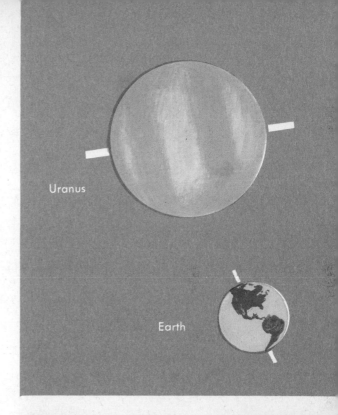

Uranus

Earth

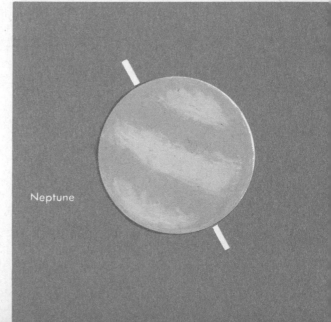

Neptune

Both Neptune and Pluto were discovered "on paper" before they were observed through a telescope.

Scientists noticed that Uranus did not follow a regular orbit. At times it seemed to be drawn off course as though attracted by some unknown planet. Scientists worked out charts which showed where such an unknown planet would be. When they turned their telescopes on the position, they saw a new planet. They named it Neptune.

Pluto was discovered this same way. Scientists suspected that there was another planet beyond Neptune when Neptune, also, seemed to follow an irregular course at times.

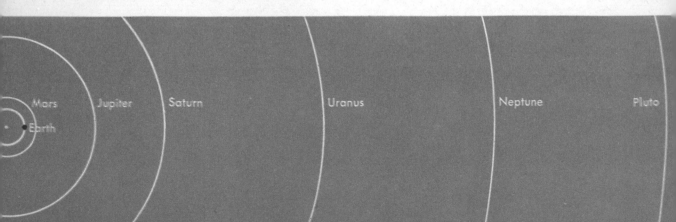

COMETS, METEORS, AND METEORITES

One of the most
thrilling sights
you may ever see is
a brilliant comet
moving across the sky. The thing you notice first is
the bright head of the comet. The head is made of
small pieces of rock, dust, and some gases. This head
seems to be burning, but it is really only reflecting
light from the sun.

41

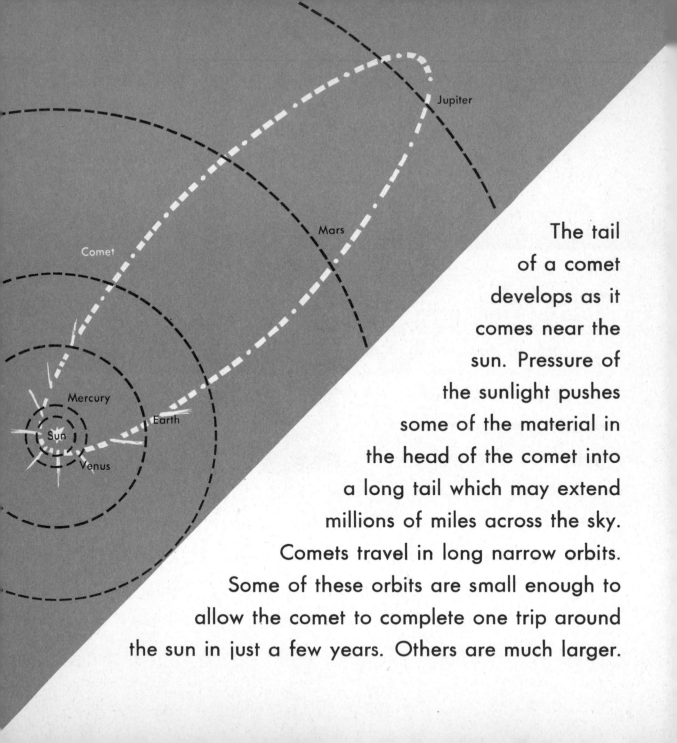

Jupiter

Mars

Comet

Mercury

Earth

Sun

Venus

The tail of a comet develops as it comes near the sun. Pressure of the sunlight pushes some of the material in the head of the comet into a long tail which may extend millions of miles across the sky. Comets travel in long narrow orbits. Some of these orbits are small enough to allow the comet to complete one trip around the sun in just a few years. Others are much larger.

Perhaps you have seen "shooting stars." These are not really stars, but meteors or stones from outer space which fall into the atmosphere of the earth. As the meteor moves swiftly through the air, it is heated until it glows white hot. The heat is usually great enough to burn most meteors to dust.

Meteors often travel in swarms. When the earth passes through one of these meteor swarms, there is a shower of meteors or "shooting stars." Most meteors weigh less than one ounce. Many are no larger than a grain of sand.

Meteors which crash to the earth are called meteorites. Luckily, not many meteorites reach the earth. The picture above shows a huge hole or crater believed to have been made by a meteorite crashing into the earth.

Some meteorites are made of iron and nickel. Others are made of stony materials.

A few meteorites are very large and weigh many tons.

Most meteorites are small stony pieces of rock.

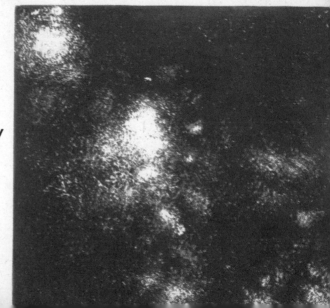

OUR SOLAR SYSTEM AND THE UNIVERSE

We have seen that our solar system is too huge for us even to imagine. But if we could stand far out in space, we would see that our sun is only a medium-sized star among a family of millions of other stars. Such a family of stars is called a galaxy

Our galaxy is called the Milky Way. It is thought to be in the shape of a giant pin wheel.

The part of the Milky Way that we can see appears to be a hazy band across the dark sky.

But the Milky Way is not the end of the universe. It is only one of a large collection of galaxies called a supergalaxy. There are billions of stars in a supergalaxy. It is thought that many supergalaxies make up our universe.

Do you think that among all these stars there could be a solar system like ours, with a planet like earth and living things as we know them?

Many people think so.

PICTURE DICTIONARY

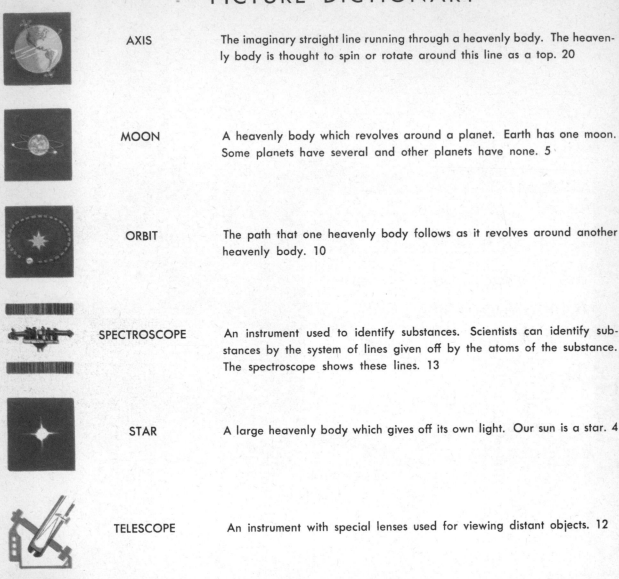

AXIS — The imaginary straight line running through a heavenly body. The heavenly body is thought to spin or rotate around this line as a top. 20

MOON — A heavenly body which revolves around a planet. Earth has one moon. Some planets have several and other planets have none. 5

ORBIT — The path that one heavenly body follows as it revolves around another heavenly body. 10

SPECTROSCOPE — An instrument used to identify substances. Scientists can identify substances by the system of lines given off by the atoms of the substance. The spectroscope shows these lines. 13

STAR — A large heavenly body which gives off its own light. Our sun is a star. 4

TELESCOPE — An instrument with special lenses used for viewing distant objects. 12

UNIVERSE — The entire collection of heavenly bodies known and unknown to man. 45

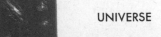